Isn't That Amazing!

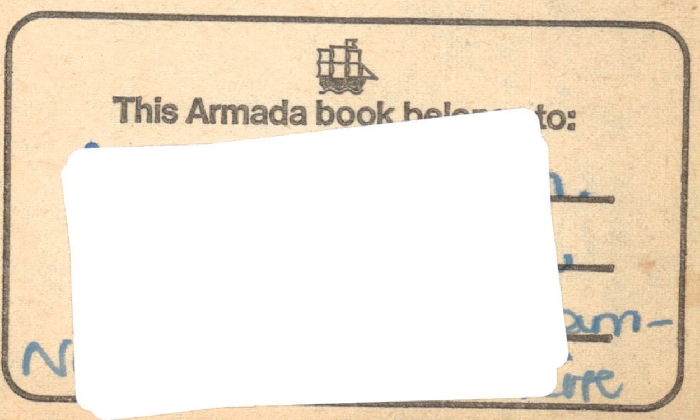

Other Armada books by Peter Eldin

The Trickster's Handbook
The Secret Agent's Handbook
The Whizzkid's Handbook
The Armada TV Quiz Book

Peter Eldin

Isn't That Amazing!

Illustrated by Juliet Stanwell-Smith

AN ARMADA ORIGINAL

Isn't That Amazing! was first published in Armada in 1979 by
Fontana Paperbacks,
14 St. James's Place, London SW1A 1PS

Printed in Great Britain by
Love & Malcomson Ltd.,
Brighton Road, Redhill, Surrey

Contents

Before We Start

This is a book about science, but science with a difference. When I was at school I was a dunce in science (I wasn't much brighter in other subjects either). I was more interested in conjuring. But as my interest in conjuring developed I found that a number of tricks were based on scientific principles, and I began to realise that science could be fun.

Over the years I have collected together a number of tricks and experiments from which I have derived a great deal of enjoyment. I have selected some of these for you to try out. I am sure that you will find them most intriguing, and that your friends will be amazed by them.

The prime function of this book is to provide you with plenty of things that you can do for fun. There has, however, also been a serious objective and that is to give you some insight into the world of science. This is a most fascinating subject, but the following pages only skim the surface, for there is science all around you, if only you will look for it.

I will be happy if I have given you some ideas on how to entertain your friends. If, however, I have inspired you to look further into the fascination of science, in all its amazing aspects, then I have achieved my objective and I will be pleased that you will not be such a dunce at the subject as I am.

Have fun.

PETER ELDIN

Experiments

1. Burst the Bag

It is often amazing how simple, everyday things that we take for granted are connected with science. Take, for instance, blowing up a bag and then bursting it. Nothing remarkable about that, is there? But have you ever stopped to wonder why it happens?

Take a paper bag and just blow it up a little. Screw up the neck of the bag so that the air cannot escape and then try to burst it by hitting it with your free hand. You may find that this is difficult, if not impossible, to achieve. Even if you are successful in bursting the bag it will not make very much noise.

Now take a similar bag and blow it up as much as you can. This compresses the air inside the bag and will produce quite a different result when you repeat the process. Screw up the neck of the bag once again and hit it with your hand. The bag will burst with a loud bang that is sure to wake up Dad who is having his afternoon snooze.

When he calms down you can explain that you were just trying out a scientific experiment. The action of hitting the bag compresses the air in the bag even more and the fabric of the bag is not strong enough to withstand the strain. It therefore bursts. The compressed air escapes in a rush and sets up vibrations in the surrounding air which you, and your dad, will hear as a loud report.

And when your dad spanks you for disturbing his slumber just try to remember that the sounds produced by his smacks are simply vibrations in the air. Isn't science fun!

2. Breezy Fingertips

Ask a friend to hold his palm up to face you. Now say that you have magic fingertips and that you can cause air to come from them.

Snap your fingers several times and then bring your hand down flat from a height. When your hand nears your friend's palm, turn your hand so that the thumb is uppermost. At this point your friend will feel a slight breeze coming from your fingertips, just as you said he would.

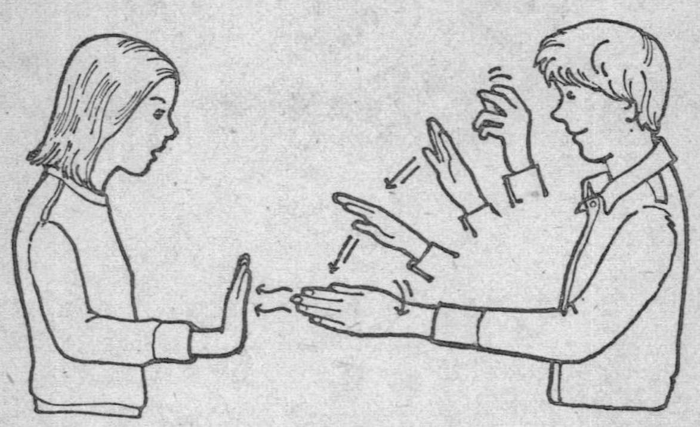

Turning your hand re-directs the downward draught

What your friend will not realise is that you have simply created a downward current of air. By turning your hand at the crucial moment you direct the current towards your friend's palm.

The clicking of the fingers at the start of the demonstration? Well, that is nothing more than a bit of showmanship, designed to make the demonstration more mysterious.

3. Defying Gravity

We all know that gravity causes things to fall to the ground if they are not supported in some way, but here is a simple experiment in which you can apparently defy the laws of gravity. All you need is a drinking straw and some water.

Completely immerse the straw so that it becomes filled with water. If you were now to lift the straw out of the water all the liquid in the straw would flow out. But if you place a finger over one end of the straw before removing it from the water and then hold it, as shown in the illustration, the water does not flow out. It appears to defy the laws of gravity—what is holding it up?

The water remains in the straw until you remove your finger

The answer to that question is air pressure, which is supporting the column of water from below, as it is greater than the pressure at the top of the straw. As soon as you remove your finger, the air pressure is equal at both ends of the straw, gravity takes over and the water flows out.

4. Straw Fountain

Having made the water stay in the straw in the last experiment, try going one step further. Show your friends the last experiment, dip the straw in some water and then place your finger over the top to prevent the water from running out as you did before. Now place the forefinger of your other hand at the bottom of the straw and turn the straw upside down. The straw is then placed back into the glass of water with your finger still on top. As soon as you remove your finger the water in the straw runs up the straw and pours out of the top like a fountain.

The amazing thing about this experiment is that when anyone else tries, and apparently does exactly the same as you, the water does not flow out of the top, it stays in exactly the same position. If your friend lifts the straw slightly the water will run down it. But no matter what he does, the water will not flow out of the top of the straw as it did for you.

The reason that it works for you and not for anyone else is that you cheat a little. When you place the straw into the water on the first occasion you apparently put your finger over the top of the straw, but, unbeknown to everyone watching, you put your finger only partway over the top of the straw so that air can still enter. Begin to lift the straw out of the glass and then put your finger completely over the top of the straw when the straw is about halfway out of the water. The finger movement you have to make is so small that no-one will notice it but it is upon this little subterfuge that the whole trick works. Continue to pull the straw out of the water, turn it upside down with your other finger on the bottom and finish the experiment as already described.

Anyone who tries to copy your feat will put their finger on top of the straw too soon and they will never get the fountain to work like that.

5. Straw of Strength

Try pushing an ordinary drinking straw into a potato. You will find that the straw will just buckle up. To enable the straw to penetrate the potato, you have to strengthen the straw. This you can do in a very simple and most amazing way. All you have to do is put your finger on the top end of the straw.

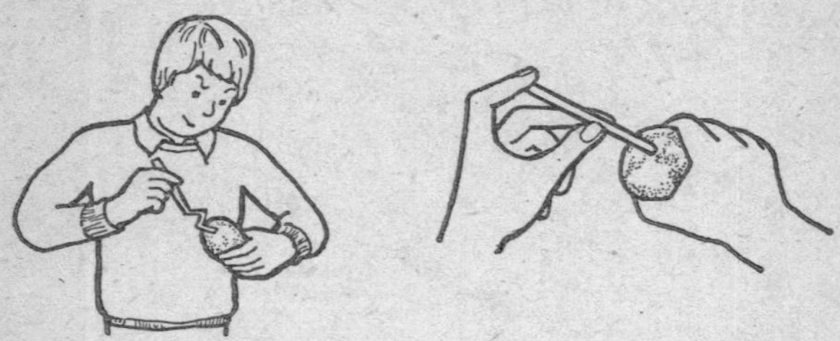

The straw will not penetrate the potato . . . until you put a finger over one end

This strengthens the straw, by preventing the air within it escaping, when the straw is pushed into the potato. The trapped air acts as an interior pillar supporting the walls of the straw. Keep your finger over the top of the straw and push it into the potato with a clean, straight thrust. This time the straw will go into the potato quite easily.

6. Flatten the Straw

Place a cherry stone, orange pip, or something similar into a glass of lemonade. Put a drinking straw into the lemonade and suck up some of the lemonade, for this experiment is tasty, as well as scientific. As you suck you create a partial vacuum inside the straw and the air pressure on the surface of the lemonade forces the liquid into the straw and then into your mouth.

Keeping one end of the straw in your mouth, place the other end of the straw on the cherry stone, sucking all the time. The cherry stone will prevent any more lemonade entering the straw. The lemonade, already in the straw, is sucked up into your mouth, which again creates a vacuum inside the straw. As a result, the air pressure is greater on the outside of the straw than it is on the inside and the straw will be pressed flat by the pressure outside.

7. Baited Breath

Put a balloon into a large bottle with a narrow neck. Stretch the neck of the balloon so that it fits over the neck of the bottle as shown in the illustration.

No matter how hard he blows, the balloon will not inflate

Now challenge anyone to blow up the balloon in the bottle. It sounds ridiculously easy and many of your friends will try to do it. But no matter how hard they try they will not succeed. Normally, when you blow up a balloon, you raise the air pressure inside it above that of the air that surrounds it, and so the balloon expands. But when you try to blow up the balloon inside the bottle, any expansion of the balloon will increase the pressure of the air in the bottle. The air in the bottle resists this increase in pressure and so the balloon is allowed to expand only slightly.

8. Blow It Out

Place a lighted candle on a table behind a large bottle. Now tell your friends that your lungs are so powerful that you can blow straight through the solid bottle and blow out the candle. They may not believe you—until you blow directly at the bottle and the candle goes out, just as you said it would.

Your breath appears to go through the bottle

What you do not tell your friends is that this is caused by your breath flowing past both sides of the bottle. This creates an area of low pressure as we have seen in some of the previous experiments. As soon as you stop blowing, air rushes in to fill the partial vacuum you have created and it is this inrush of air that snuffs the flame.

9. Wrong Way Flame

The flame bends the wrong way!

Now try a similar experiment, but this time hold a sheet of card up in front of the lighted candle. Blow steadily and the flame of the candle will lean towards you—and not away, as most people will expect.

Once again, it is the reduction in air pressure that does the work. As in the previous experiment, an area of low pressure is formed, this time behind the card. Air moves in to fill the partial vacuum you have created and it blows the candle flame towards you.

10. The Power of Attraction

Attach a length of cotton to each of two ping pong balls. The easiest way to do this is to use a short piece of sticky tape. Tie the upper ends of the threads to a ruler. They should be about three centimetres apart.

Hold the ruler and ask a friend to blow through a drinking straw from a few centimetres away. He is to aim his puff exactly between the two balls.

You might expect the balls to be blown apart—but they do exactly the opposite! The explanation is similar to that of the previous experiments. Blowing between the balls reduces the air pressure and the normal pressure on the outside of the spheres pushes them together.

Another way to demonstrate the same principle is to hold two long strips of newspaper, one in each hand, and blow down between them. The papers will be drawn together, no matter how hard you may try to blow them apart.

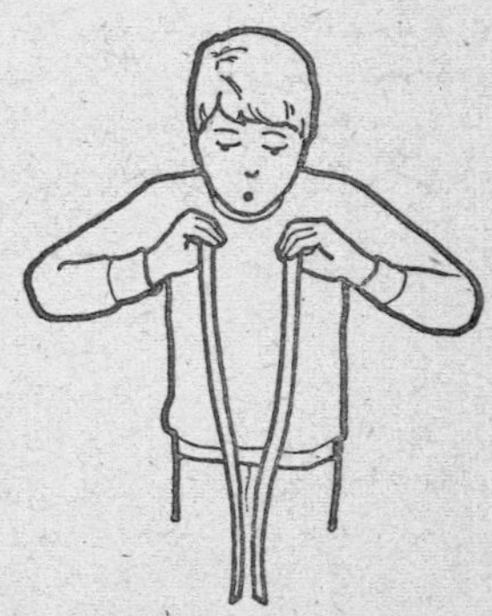

Blow—and the papers move together

11. Rising Water

Place a lighted candle in the centre of a soup bowl. Use some drips of wax from the candle, or a blob of plasticine, to secure the base of the candle so that it will not fall over. Now fill the soup bowl with water. Place a milk bottle over the burning candle and watch what happens. You will see the water from the bowl begin to move up inside the bottle and it will continue to rise until the candle goes out.

As the candle burns so the water rises

The explanation for this amazing happening is that as the candle burns it uses up all of the oxygen inside the bottle. As a result, the remaining parts of air left inside the bottle take up less room and create a partial vacuum. This allows the outside air pressing on the surface of the water in the bowl to push the water up into the milk bottle.

If you are really observant you will realise that the water rises about one fifth of the way up the bottle. This is due to the fact that oxygen comprises one fifth of air.

12. Limpet Glass

Take a narrow plastic tumbler or a light egg cup and fill it to the top with water. Place your hand over the top of the glass and press down so that the glass fits neatly into the palm of your hand. Now straighten your hand and move it upwards. Surprise, surprise, the tumbler comes too—stuck to your hand like a limpet.

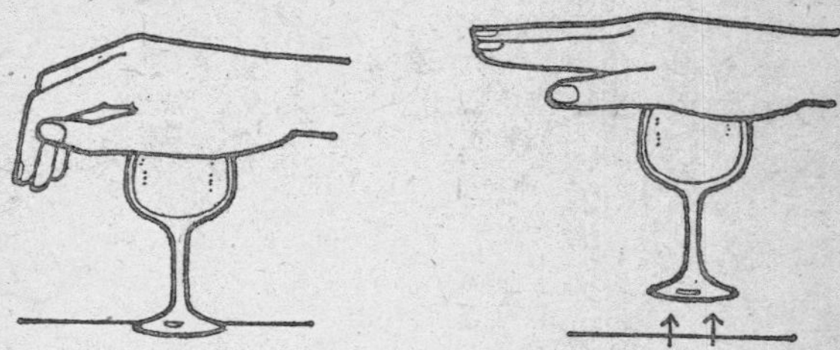

Lift your hand . . . and the glass comes too!

The reason this happens is that when you press down on top of the tumbler you exclude all the air between the palm of your hand and the surface of the water. It is air pressure and not magic that accomplishes this baffling feat.

Like all the other experiments in this book, you should try this out in private first. This particular item requires some practice before you will be able to get it right. It helps if you have large hands, for the palm must cover the whole area of the tumbler.

If you hear a slight hiss of air as you raise your hand, it means that air is leaking out between your hand and the surface, so try it again.

13. Expanding Balloon

Take an ordinary balloon and blow it up. Do not blow it up as far as it will go but make sure that there is sufficient air in the balloon to give it some shape. Tie the neck of the balloon to prevent the air escaping.

Now hold the balloon near a warm radiator. As if by magic, the balloon will get larger and larger. If you hold it near the radiator for too long it may expand so much that it will eventually burst.

This happens because heat causes air to expand. The air inside the balloon tries to expand, but, as it is confined within the balloon, it causes the balloon to grow.

14. Diving Match

Break two or three matches in half and keep the halves with the heads. Place these half matches in a bottle that has a thin neck and then fill the bottle to the top with water. Press your thumb on to the top of the bottle and the matches will sink to the bottom. Release the pressure and they will rise to the surface once again. With practice you will be able to control the rate of descent and ascent by varying the pressure of your thumb.

As you press with your thumb you are increasing the pressure of water on the small bubbles of air within the fibres of the matches. This pressure causes the air to take up less room and as a result the matches become denser than water and sink to the bottom. When you release the pressure, the air is allowed to expand, and the matches become less dense and float to the top.

15. Another Diver

To make this diver you will need a small eye dropper, a milk bottle or jar filled to the brim with water, a sheet of rubber (an old balloon will do), and an elastic band.

Put the eye dropper into the water and squeeze the rubber bulb so that some of the air is pressed out and water is taken into the dropper. Put the dropper in the water and eject some of the water from inside it until it is heavy enough to float with the rubber bulb just reaching the surface. Place the sheet of rubber over the top of the jar and hold it in place with the elastic band.

To make the dropper sink, press on the rubber, and to make it rise to the surface, take your hand off the rubber. It works in exactly the same way as the diving matches in the previous experiment. As you press on the rubber you compress the air inside the dropper to make it less buoyant. When you release the pressure, the air expands again and the dropper rises to the surface.

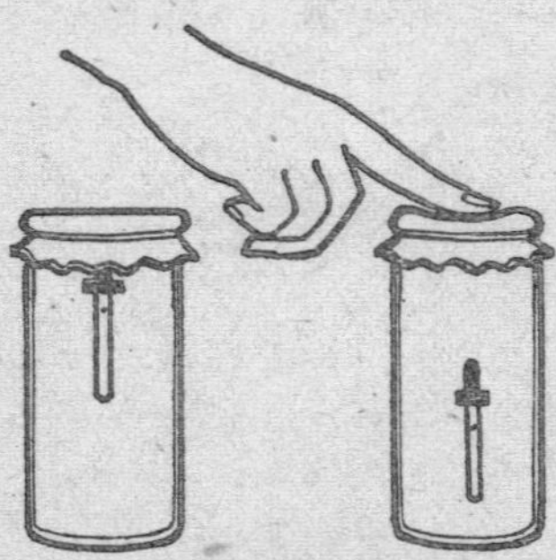

When you increase the pressure the diver goes down

16. Tumbler Transportation

Wet the rim of a glass tumbler and stand it upside-down on a smooth wet surface that is slightly inclined. Now light a candle and bring the flame near to the side of the tumbler at the top. It appears that the glass cannot stand the heat, for it will immediately begin to slide away down the incline.

The tumbler moves on a cushion of warm air

As we have already seen, heating air causes it to expand and that is the real explanation for the tumbler's transportation. As the candle heats the air inside the glass, the air expands and lifts the glass slightly, so that it rests upon the layer of water you placed around the rim. This enables it to slide down the incline. You will often see the same thing happen when glasses have been washed in hot water and then placed on a sloping draining board.

17. Rotating Fan

Take a foil top from a milk bottle and cut eight slits in it from the outside to near the centre. Give a slight twist to each of the divisions you have just made and then push a pencil into the centre, just enough to make a small dent. You should now be able to balance the foil on the tip of the pencil, as shown in the illustration.

Rising warm air causes the fan to turn

Place a candle by the side of the pencil and the foil will begin to rotate like a fan. It does this because the air beneath it has been heated by the flame of the candle. Hot air is lighter than cool air and so it rises. As it rises it pushes the blade of your fan around. It should be noted that each of the twists should be in the same direction to make this experiment work.

The little fans that create the flickering effect found on coal-effect gas and electric fires work in the same way. In this instance it is the heat produced by a red light bulb that causes the rotary movement.

18. Floating the Currency

This experiment can be performed only with certain currencies, so be sure to try it out in private before showing it to your friends. The only coins that can be used for this demonstration are foreign coins that are made of a light aluminium alloy.

From your friend's point of view all you do is take a coin and float it on the surface of the water. What they do not realise is that the coin has been specially selected for the demonstration and that there is a thin film on the surface of water (due to its contact with the air). This film is known as 'surface tension'. It is this film that supports the coin.

If you are unable to find a coin that is suitable for this experiment you will discover that it can also be done with one of dad's old razor blades. If you use a razor blade, however, please make sure that you do not cut yourself.

Whether you use a coin or a razor blade it is as well to place it very carefully upon the surface of the water. One way that you can do this is to first place the object to be used (it can also be done with a pin or a needle) on a small piece of tissue paper and float this in the surface first. Use your fingers to push the paper beneath the surface and the coin, razor blade, or pin will remain floating on the surface.

You can improve your chances of success with these experiments by rubbing the coin or what-have-you with candle wax, or simply between your hands, before you float it on the water.

19. Paper Boat

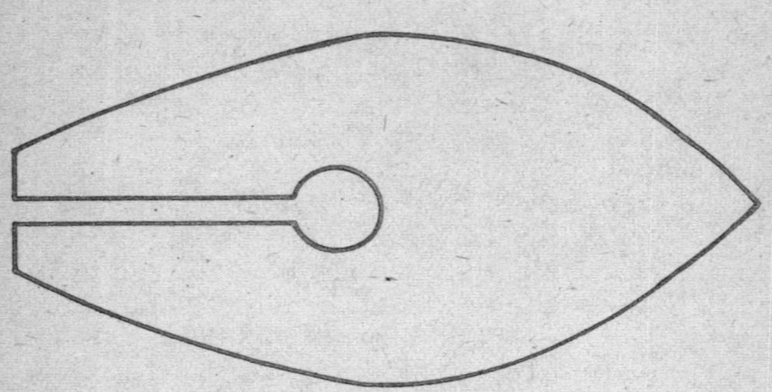

A boat powered by washing up liquid

From a sheet of thin card cut out the boat shape shown in the drawing. Lay it carefully on the surface of a large bowl of water.

Allow a few drops of washing-up liquid, or any similar liquid, to drop into the triangle cut out at the rear of the boat. The oil tries to spread across the surface of the water, but is prevented from doing so by the paper. There is only one way for the oil to escape and that is through the narrow opening at the rear of the boat.

As the oil flows out it causes the boat to move forward, in accordance with Newton's third law of motion, which states that for every action there is an equal and opposite reaction. As the liquid moves backwards the paper boat is forced forward.

20. Mothball Motor

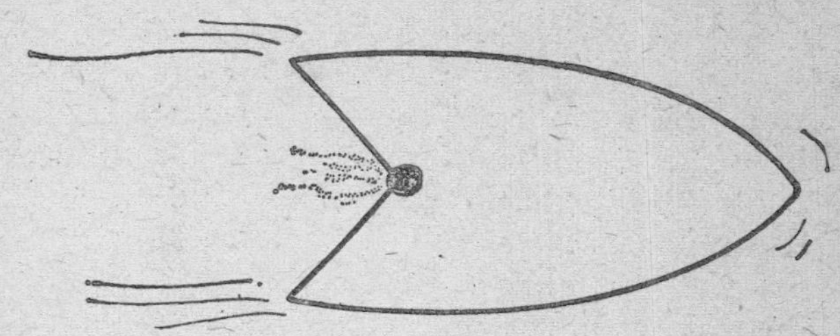

Camphor releases the surface tension and the boat is pulled forward

Make the outline of a boat from a piece of thin card as shown in the illustration. In the centre of the V-shaped stern glue a piece of camphor. The easiest way to obtain camphor is to ask your mother for a camphor mothball out of the wardrobe.

Place the boat on the surface of some water and watch it go. This happens because there is a thin film on the surface of the water, known as surface tension, that exerts a pull. As the camphor dissolves in the water it breaks up this film, so that the surface tension, or pull, is greater at the front than at the rear and the boat moves forward, just as the paper boat did in the previous experiment.

21. Hydrostatic Glass

Place a sheet of dampened paper over the rim of a glass full of water and it will remain in place even though the glass is turned upside down. This is due to atmospheric pressure and, as such, is a straightforward demonstration of a scientific principle. You can, however, make the demonstration much more interesting by adding a touch of magic.

Before the demonstration, place a disc of glass or plastic on the paper to be used. This disc must be of the same diameter as the mouth of the glass that you intend to use.

Show the glass and fill it with water. Now pick up the sheet of paper and, at the same time, secretly pick up the disc of plastic. Dip both into the water you are using and then place the paper (and the disc) over the mouth of the glass. Care must be taken at this stage to ensure that the disc is in the right position over the mouth of the glass.

Now turn the glass over but keep your hand against the paper so that it does not fall. Slowly remove your hand

Water that appears to defy the laws of gravity

and show the paper preventing the water from flowing out of the glass. This experiment is well known to many people so there will be little exclamation at this point. You could, in fact, explain that the paper remains in place due to atmospheric pressure. Then peel the paper away and the water apparently remains in the glass. This is again due to hydrostatic pressure but, as the plastic disc cannot be seen, it appears to be real magic.

It is as well to practise this trick over a sink to start with just in case you have an accident. To achieve a better seal between the disc and the tumbler it is worthwhile smearing a layer of vaseline on the surface of the disc.

22. Sticky Water

Use a strip of adhesive tape to attach one end of a length of string to a table tennis ball.

Turn on the kitchen tap to provide a good steady flow of water. Hold the top of the string so that the ball hangs a few centimetres away from the stream of water. Now swing the ball towards the water. Instead of swinging back, as you might expect, the ball remains touching the column of water. You will even find that you can pull the ball up the water almost to the top.

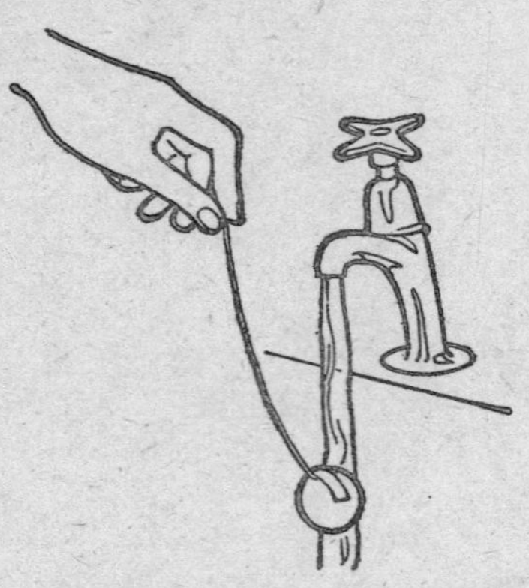

The ball is attracted to the water

This happens because the stream of water rushing against the ball creates less pressure than the air pressure on the other side. With the low pressure attracting the ball and the air pressure pushing against the ball, it is drawn automatically to the column of water, as you will find when you try the experiment for yourself.

23. Watering Can

Find a long tin can and use a hammer and nail to punch three or four holes down one side. Now put the can under a running tap and watch the water run out of the holes. Being a scientist, you will observe that the water running out of the lowest holes streams out further than that coming from the uppermost hole, and you will obviously wonder why that should be the case.

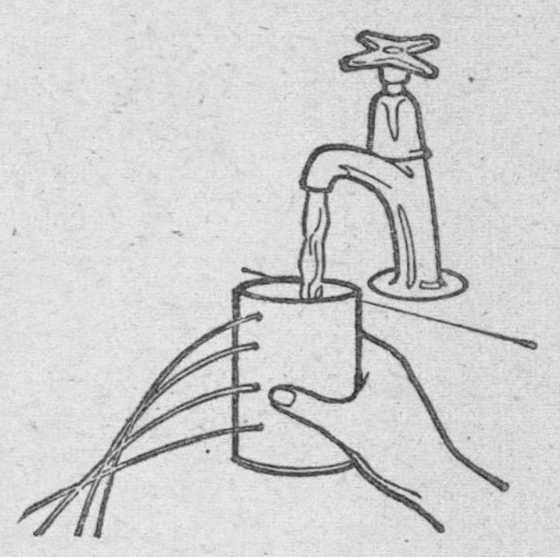

Water pressure is greatest at the bottom

To understand why this happens, take another tin can, a jam jar, or something similar and try to push it downwards into a bowl of water. Can you feel the water resisting your downward push? This is the pressure exerted by the water. It is rather like air pressure, for it presses on an object from all sides. If you push the jam jar further down into the water you will be able to feel an increase in the resistance. This is because the pressure is greater the deeper you go. And that is why the bottom stream of water coming out of the can, in the experiment we have just tried, comes out further than the water at the top—the water pressure is greater at the bottom of the can and it pushes the water out faster.

24. Magdeburg Sink Plungers

Borrow the plunger that you use to unblock the sink and press it down hard on a clean wet surface. Now try to pull it free. It's not easy, is it? The reason is that in pressing the plunger down you forced out most of the air that was inside the cone and created a partial vacuum. This means that the outside air pressure is greater than that inside the plunger so more effort is required to move it.

An even more impressive version of the same experiment can be done with two such plungers. Having wetted the mouths of the plungers, place one directly against the mouth of the other and squeeze the two together to express as much air as possible. You will probably need a friend to help you to do this. You will certainly need his help for the next part, for you now have to try to pull the plungers apart, and you will find this extremely difficult. Once again it is the force of atmospheric pressure that prevents you from doing this.

With the second of these plunger experiments you were

They will not pull apart

emulating the German scientist, Otto von Guericke, who demonstrated the same thing in 1654 at Magdeburg. He did it in slightly more spectacular fashion for he used two iron hemispheres about 55 centimetres in diameter. Their rims were placed together, covered in grease to ensure a good seal, and all the air removed from inside. To get the spheres apart, von Guericke had to employ the services of two teams of eight horses pulling in opposite directions. It just goes to show how strong air pressure can be!

25. Tumbler Suspension

Here is another version of von Guericke's experiment you can try. This one looks like real magic and you can show it as such to your friends.

Light a small piece of a candle and place it inside a glass tumbler. On top of this tumbler place a piece of card that has been saturated with water, and on top of this, mouth down, place another tumbler exactly the same as the first so the set-up looks like that shown in the illustration.

Lift one glass and the other comes as well

Eventually the candle will use up all of the oxygen in the lower tumbler and will go out. As a result the air in the tumblers will be rarified and you will find that if you lift the top tumbler the lower one will adhere to it, as the outside pressure of the air is holding them both together. You do not have to tell your friends this. Just tell them that you are a great magician. They may believe you.

26. Siphon It

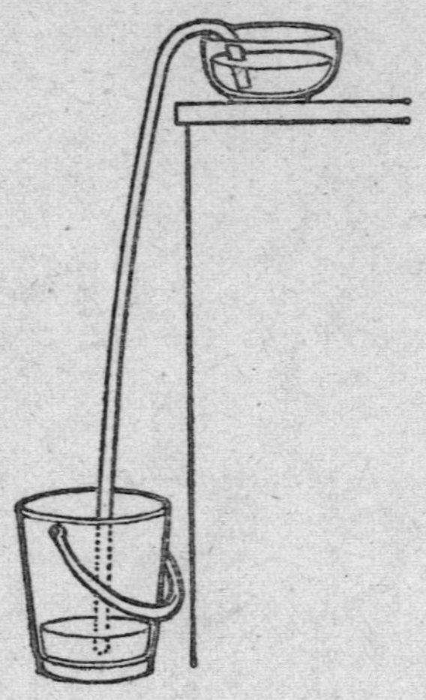

A simple siphon

For this experiment you will need a length of rubber tubing or a short piece of garden hose. Put some water in a bowl in your kitchen sink and place a bucket on the floor. Now fill the rubber tubing with water by immersing it in the bowl. Pinch one end of the tubing between your fingers so that the water does not run out and carefully place this end into the bucket. Water will now run out of the bowl and into the bucket—so before you try this experiment make sure that you have a bucket that is large enough to take all of the water from your bowl. Your mother will not think much of your scientific experiments if you flood her kitchen with water.

A siphon like this works because as the water flows out

of the tube something has to fill the void that it leaves. As the top end of the tube is under water the void is filled by water. The air pressure acting on the surface of the bowl continually pushes more water into the tube. This will continue until the bowl is empty.

27. Plant Waterer

An automatic plant-watering system

This is a handy method for watering household plants when you go away on holiday. It is also fascinating and, of course, demonstrates a scientific principle.

Place a bowl of water near the plant pot but at a higher level. Roll a piece of rag into a rope and place it over the edge of the bowl so that one end is in the water and the other end is touching the soil in the plant pot. The water from the bowl will rise up the rag and drip into the pot and will keep the plant adequately watered for quite a long time. With several pieces of rag coming from the bowl you could water quite a number of plants.

This happens due to a phenomenon called 'capillary action', which is the attraction between the molecules that make up the water and those of the rag. As the water is attracted to the molecules of the rag it creeps along the rag and eventually drops out into the plant pot. Capillary action is also the reason why blotting paper soaks up ink.

28. Prawn Power

How can you use a prawn or a shrimp to empty a glass of water?

That may sound like a strange question but, in fact, the answer is quite straightforward—capillary action.

Fill a wine glass with water and then position a large prawn or shrimp so that it hangs over the rim of a glass like the rag in the previous experiment.

As in the previous experiment, capillary action will force the water up through the prawn and out of the glass.

The prawn 'drinks' up the water!

29. Stick-together Corks

Show your friends seven ordinary wine-bottle corks and a bowl of water and challenge them to place the corks in the water so that they float upright.

When your friends try this they will find that, no matter

Immerse the corks . . . and capillary action holds them together

how hard they try to keep them upright, the corks will always fall over and float on their sides.

You can, however, make them float upright by using science. All you have to do is hold the corks together in a bunch and dip them under the water for a few seconds. As soon as the corks are completely wet, bring them to the surface and then release your grip—the corks will stay together and they will be floating upright.

This fascinating feat is accomplished by capillary action—the water creeping between the corks holds them together.

30. Ironing with Science

Ask your mother how she would get a grease stain off clothing and she will probably tell you that she would first place a piece of absorbent brown paper over the stain and then rub over it with a hot iron. You can now baffle her with your expert scientific knowledge by explaining that she has just demonstrated the remarkable fact of capillary action. The heat from the iron melts the grease on the clothing and the paper soaks it up by means of capillary action.

How to remove grease stains

31. Half and Half

Pick a white flower, such as a carnation, and split the stalk in half from the bottom up for about ten centimetres. Place one half of the stem into a jar of water to which you have added a quantity of red ink. Place the other part of the stem into another jar of water to which has been added some blue ink. To stop the flower from falling over you may have to support it by taping it to a piece of card or tying it to a stick. Leave the flower for several hours, or overnight.

When you look at the flower the following morning, you will have quite a surprise, for one half of the flower will be blue and the other half red! The two liquids have risen all the way up the stem to the head of the flower. If you are

Half is red and half is blue

really clever you could try another version of the experiment in which the stem is cut into four and each portion put into different colours so that you can have a flower of four colours.

Once again, capillary action is responsible for this remarkable feat.

32. Sucker Trick

For this experiment you will need a radish, a knife, and a small plate or a saucer. Cut the radish in two and then scoop out a small amount from the centre of one of the cut surfaces, being careful not to cut the edge of the radish.

Press the cut face of the radish on to the plate. With a bit of luck, and provided you have cut the radish exactly, when you pick up the radish the plate will come too.

It happens as a result of suction and capillary action but it is as well to do the experiment over a soft surface—just in case!

33. Curious Curve

Place two sheets of clean glass together as shown in the illustration. Tape them together, but first place a couple of strips of cardboard down one edge so that the sheets of glass are closer together on one side than they are on the other.

Now place the lower edge of the two sheets into a shallow bowl of water to which some vegetable dye has been added. The water will rise up between the panes of glass, but the closer the sheets are together the higher the water will rise. It thus forms itself into a curved formation that looks most intriguing.

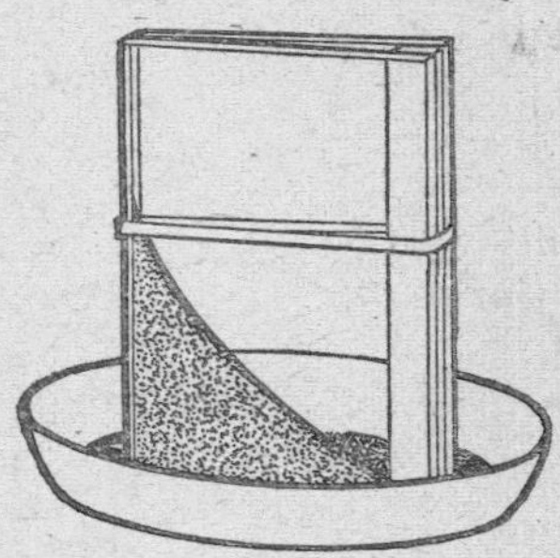

How the curve appears

The water does this because of the attraction between it and the sides of the glass that enables it to climb up the glass by means of capillary action. It rises highest where the glass is closed, because the weight of water between the glass at that point is less than where the glass sheets are further apart.

34. Create a Rainbow

Fill a bowl with water and then rest a mirror at an angle against one side of the bowl. Now direct the beam of a torch at the mirror and hold a sheet of white card next to the torch. You may have to adjust the positions of the torch and the card, but eventually you will be able to see all the colours of the rainbow projected on to the card.

If you do not have a torch handy you can achieve the same effect on a sunny day by using the sun as a light source. To achieve best results on this occasion you will have to cut a hole in another piece of card. Use this card to direct the sun's rays on to the mirror.

If you position the mirror correctly you can use the wall of the room in which you are conducting the experiment to act as the screen instead of using a sheet of card.

This experiment proves that ordinary white light is in fact made up of several different colours.

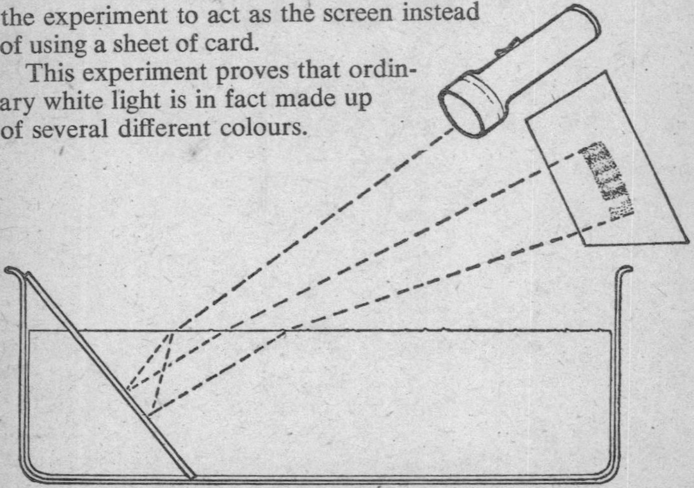

The card will reflect the colours of the rainbow

35. Hollow Candle

Push a screw into the bottom of a candle, or wrap a length of wire around it, and then float the candle in a jar of water. If the screw you have picked is not too heavy the candle should float upright in the water. Light the candle and you have an effective and safe night light.

If you leave the candle burning for a long time a remarkable thing begins to happen. The candle does not get appreciably shorter, as would normally be the case, but the flames moves down inside the candle. Eventually you will end up with a hollow candle that you can show off to your friends.

Only wax in the centre melts

The candle burns in this curious way because the water cools the outside of the candle and prevents it from melting. Only the wax in the centre melts to keep the wick fuelled—and you have a hollow candle. (Incidentally, the melted wax fuels the flame by moving up the wick through capillary action—just thought you might like to know.)

36. All Change

Fill a glass tumbler with water to which has been added some vegetable colouring, or ink. Fill a similar glass to the rim with cooking oil. Now place a small sheet of card over the mouth of the water-filled glass. Press the card close to the rim of the glass and then turn the glass upside down. Position the inverted glass exactly on top of the other glass and get someone to pull the card away gently. If you are careful you will not spill any of the water or the oil but it is as well to perform this experiment over the sink, just in case.

Move the glasses gently and soon you will see the two liquids begin to change places. The water is denser than cooking oil and so gravity draws it into the lower glass whilst the oil rises into the top one.

Don't forget to wash the glasses thoroughly after use or the person who next drinks out of them will not think very highly of your scientific experiments.

37. Bottle Fountain

For this experiment you will need a small bottle, a cork to fit the bottle, a drinking straw, a large jar that will completely cover the bottle, a plate, and some paper.

Three-quarters fill the small bottle with water. Then put in the cork through which you have already made a hole just big enough to take the straw. Push the straw into the cork so that it almost reaches the bottom of the bottle and sticks out a centimetre or so above the cork, as in the illustration.

Dampen the paper and lay it on the plate. Put the prepared bottle on the plate also and you are nearly ready.

Hold the jar upside down over a low flame, such as a candle or a low gas jet, until the air inside the jar is nice and warm. Alternatively, you can fill the jar with warm air

The fountain in action

from a hair dryer. Quickly place the jar over the bottle and watch what happens.

When air is heated, like that contained in the jar, it expands, which means that the jar now contains less air than it did originally. As it cools down it will contract. Normally this would mean that more air would be drawn into the jar to replace that which was pushed out when the jar was heated. But the damp paper on the plate prevents any air getting into the jar and so the air pressure in the jar is reduced. The air pressure in the top of the bottle, however, remains normal and it pushes the water up through the straw to produce an attractive fountain.

If you watch for the water moving up the straw you can make a mystic pass at the appropriate moment and pretend that you have started the fountain by magic.

38. String Them Along

Tie about a metre of string around a heavy book. Use only one knot and position the book so that it is near the middle of the length of string.

Now challenge a friend (pick the strongest one you know) to pull on both ends of the string and lift the book until the two halves of the string form a straight horizontal line.

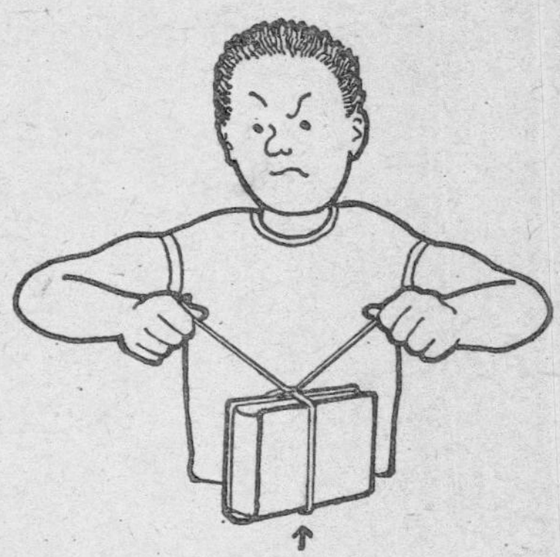

He will never counteract the downward force

Try as he may, he will not be able to achieve this apparently simple feat. In fact, it is more likely that the string will break before the horizontal line is achieved.

Once again, science is the reason that this cannot be done. The greater the angle formed between your friend's hands and the book, the less likely is he to achieve his objective. However straight he may pull the string, he can never balance the downwards force produced by the book with the two horizontal forces produced by his hands.

39. Travelling Coin

Place a playing card over the mouth of a small glass tumbler. Put a coin on the centre of the card.

Bend your forefinger down so that its nail touches the top of your thumb. Snap your forefinger forward so that it hits the edge of the card. The card will shoot away and the coin will fall into the glass.

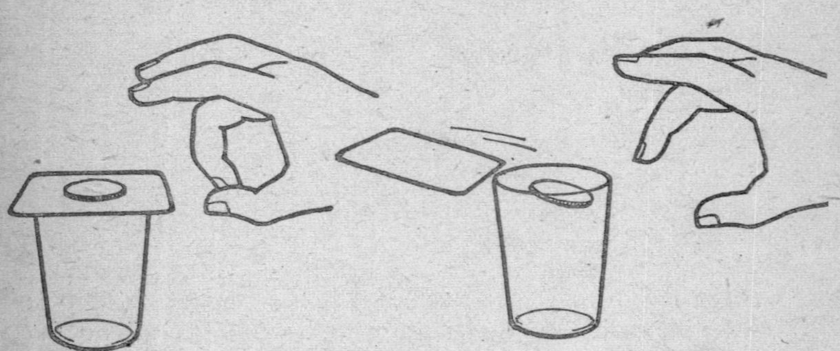

Flick the card away . . . and the coin drops into the glass

Most people expect the coin to shoot off with the card, but this does not happen. The reason is due to the scientific fact that stationary objects will remain so until some force or action makes them move. If the card was moved slowly the coin would move along with it, due to friction between the coin and the card. But, because the card is flicked fast, the frictional force is soon overcome, and so very little of the card's movement is transmitted to the coin. As a result, the card flies away and the coin remains in the same position, the force of gravity causing it to drop down into the glass.

40. Quick Flick

A quick flick of the card . . . but the coin remains in position

This is rather similar to the last experiment and works for the same reason.

Balance a card on a friend's thumb and forefinger and place a coin on the centre of the card. Now challenge him to take the card away without moving the coin. He will not be able to do it, for as soon as he moves the card the coin will move with it. To do the trick, all you have to do is flick away the card with your thumb and forefinger, as in the last experiment, and the card flies quickly away whilst the coin remains in the same position.

41. Tower of Strength

Place eight draughts in a pile on a table. If you take a ruler, and use it to give a sharp knock at the bottom draught, will the pile topple over?

The best way to discover the answer to that question is to try the experiment for yourself.

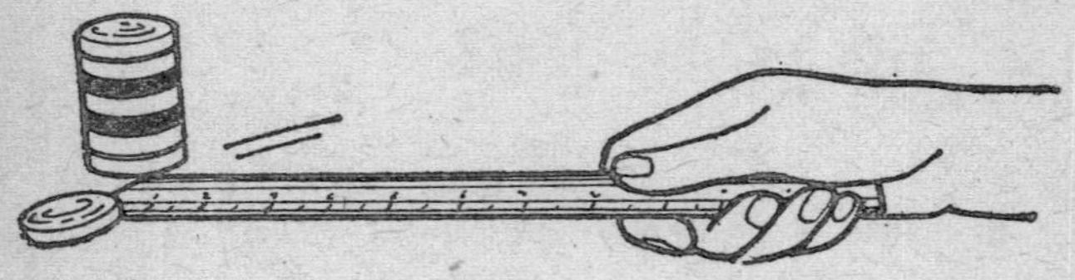

Knock the draughts away one at a time

You will see that the bottom draught will be knocked away and the rest of the pile will drop down but remain intact. As with the previous experiment, it is inertia that causes the feat to be possible.

Swing the ruler again and knock out the next draught and see how long you can continue doing this. You will find that the fewer draughts there are the more likely it is that the pile will move. This is because the force needed to move an object is related to its mass (the quantity of matter in an object). The lower the mass the lower the force required to move it.

42. Move Along

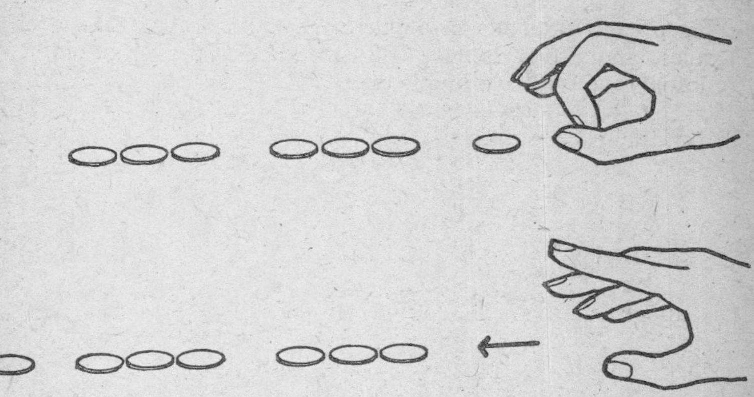

Hit the odd coin . . . and the force is transmitted along the row

Place seven coins in a long line on a smooth table top in two groups of three, and with one odd coin. With the forefinger and thumb of one hand, flick the single coin so that it hits the first group of three. Immediately, the third coin in the first group will jump to the second group, and the third coin of the second group will jump away to stand by itself.

Although the centre coins of each group remain unmoved, the impulse created by the movement of the first coin is passed along the group to the end coin of each group so that this surprising effect is achieved.

It is as well to practise this effect in advance, on the table top that you propose to use, in order to determine the correct amount of space to leave between each group of coins.

43. Keep On Spinning

Spin a hard-boiled egg and then, with one finger, stop it for just a second. When you remove your finger the egg will, as you would expect, remain stationary.

Now try the same thing with a raw egg. Spin it on the table and then stop it just for a second. When you remove your finger the egg will continue to spin, provided that you have not stopped it for too long.

The reason that this happens is that the liquid inside the egg continues spinning for a while, even though the shell is being held stationary. As soon as you release your hold the spinning liquid causes the shell to spin also.

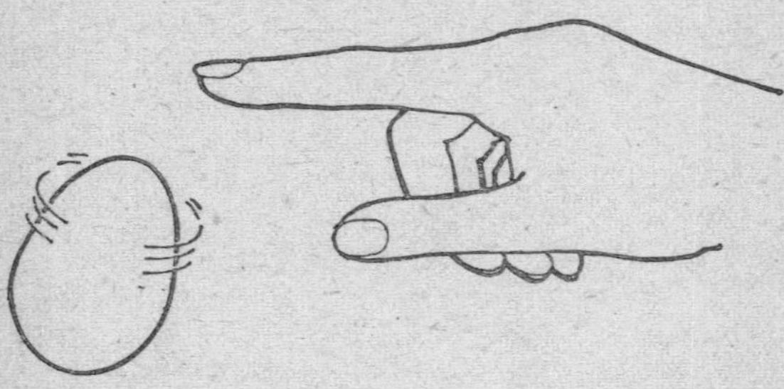

The egg will go on spinning after you have stopped it

44. The Strong Pound

Ask one of your friends to hold a pencil out in front of him with one end in each hand. Tell him to hold it firmly as you are going to hit it rather hard in just a moment. Now take a pound note or, if you are not that rich, a sheet of paper the same size as a pound note, and hit its lower edge against the pencil a couple of times. On the third time, you hit the pencil really hard with the pound note and the pencil breaks!

This feat is part science and part trickery. The crafty part lies in the fact that, unbeknown to your friend, you extend your forefinger out behind the pound note on the third strike. The impact of your finger, plus the inertia in the pencil, added by the fact that it is prevented from moving because your friend is holding it, causes the pencil to break quite easily.

45. Breaking Point

Tie a piece of strong string around a heavy book. Next, tie a length of thinner string to the first string at the top, and another piece at the bottom of the book. Tie the top string around a beam or a door knob so that the book hangs down, as in the illustration.

If you now grasp the lower string and give it a quick, sharp tug, which of the two strings will break? Which

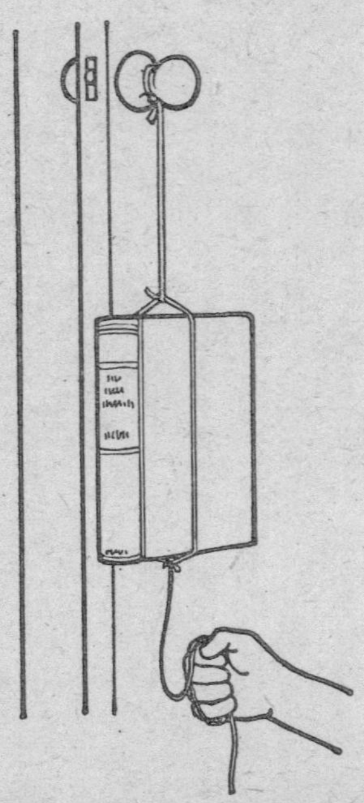

Which string will break?

string will break if you pull with gradually increasing force? Try it and see.

When you do try this experiment you will find that the sharp tug will break the lower string. This is because inertia restrains the book from moving and so you are tugging against the weight of the book. If, however, you pull smoothly, the weight of the book is working to your advantage, and against the upper string, which will break.

46. Blow the Man Down

Make a thin tube of paper or card and paste strips of paper over one end of it to give it a rounded end. Do the same at the other end, but glue a marble into this end first.

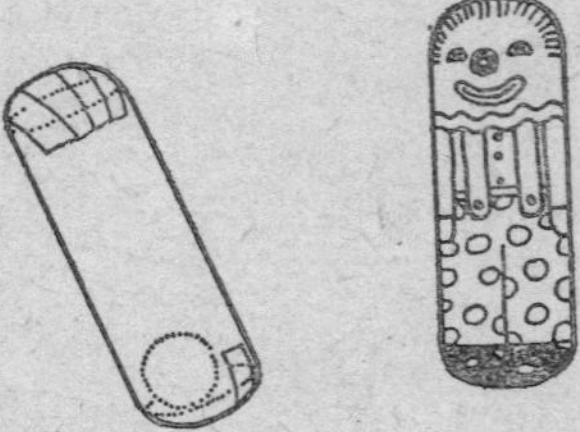

A little man that will not lie down

The tube you have made will not lie down. When you press it down it immediately stands upright again because the marble gives the tube a very low centre of gravity. If you painted the tube to look like a soldier or a clown it would make an amusing toy.

47. Roll Up, Roll Up

Here is another amazing effect accomplished by lowering an object's centre of gravity.

Make two cones out of paper or thin card and tape them together.

Place two sticks on a table with their ends resting on a thick book. The top ends of the sticks should be wider apart than the ends on the table.

Put the two cones on the lower ends of the stick and they will appear to roll uphill. It looks most uncanny.

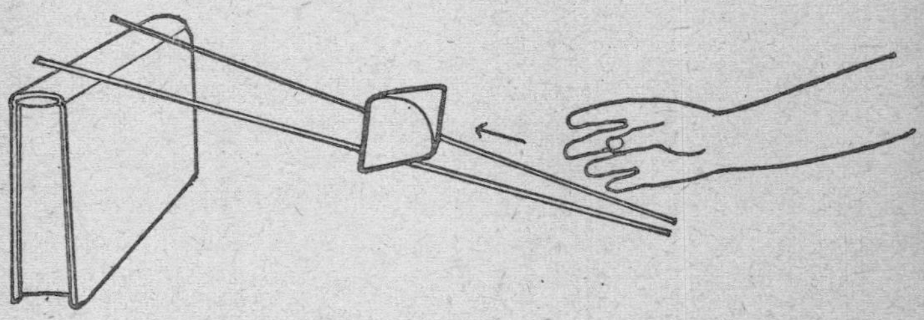

Cones that defy gravity

The spread of the two sticks causes the axis, and the centre of gravity, of the two cones to move to a lower position. Although they appear to be moving upwards the cones are, in reality, going downhill.

48. Up the Hill

This experiment is rather similar to the previous one and, again, depends upon the centre of gravity not being where most people would expect it to be.

You will need a round box, a cheese box would be ideal, or a tin. Tape a marble inside the box and then put the lid back on. Make a small pencil mark on the outside of the box so that you know the position of the marble.

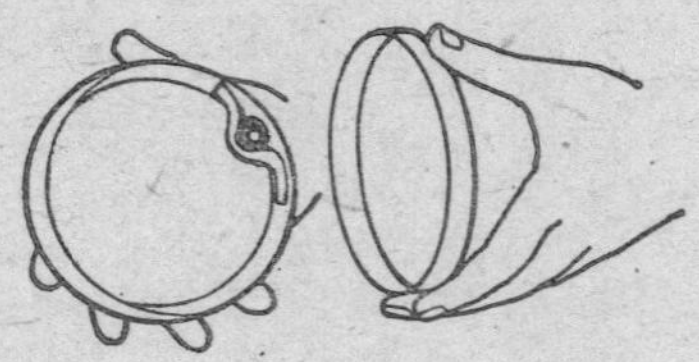

The hidden marble

Lean a book against another one to make a slope and hold the box halfway up the slope. The pencil mark should be in the position shown in the first diagram below. When you let go of the box it will roll downhill as everyone expects.

Put the box on the slope again but this time position the mark as in the second diagram below. This time, because the weight is near the top of the box, the box rolls up the slope. In both cases the weight obeys the laws of gravity and moves down but the difference in the result is quite surprising.

Another trick you can do with this magic box is to make it obey your commands. Place it on a flat surface with the weight positioned to one side near the top. Roll

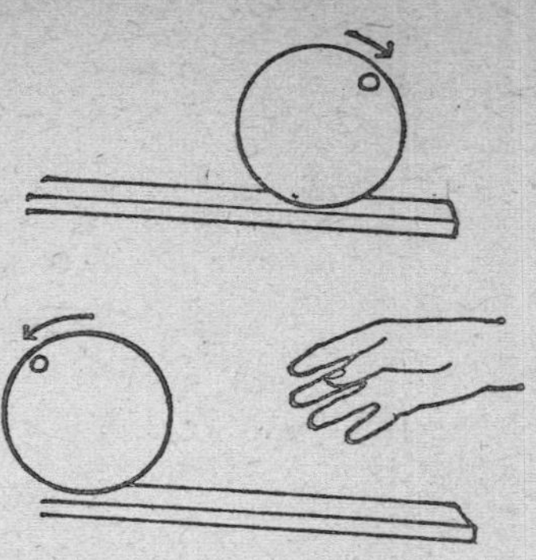

How the marble is positioned to make the box roll down or up

the box away from you, for a short distance, so that the weight moves around to near the top again but on the side opposite to that from which it started. You will have to practise this until you can position the weight correctly each time.

With practice you can command the box to change direction

When the box reaches the end of its roll the weight will move back down. As soon as this is about to happen you call, 'Come here'—and the box rolls back towards you in response to your command.

49. It's a Pushover

Even your own body can be used to show how a changing centre of gravity affects balance. Place a small object, such as a toy brick or a matchbox, on the floor and then crouch down in front of it. Now place one hand through your legs and push the object as far away as you possibly can. The movement must be a smooth action—and your finger should remain touching the object throughout the action—and you must not move your feet from their original position. That may sound easy enough, but can you now return to an upright position without moving your feet and without placing either of your hands on the floor or furniture to gain assistance?

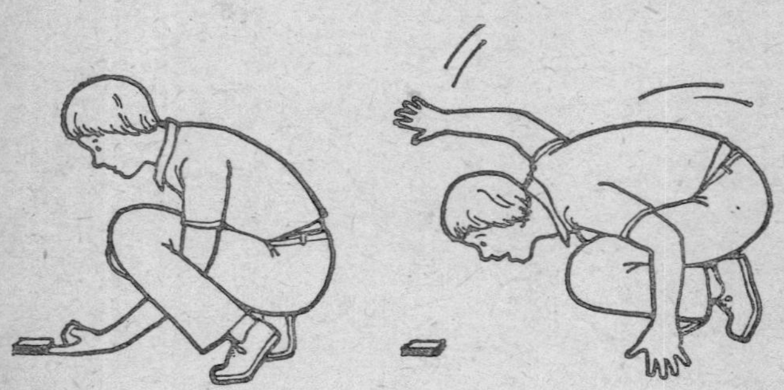

Push the matchbox . . . and over you go!

No doubt you found this extremely difficult, if not impossible, and it is more than likely that you fell over in the attempt. This happens because the peculiar position you have taken up has changed the position of your centre of gravity. There is, however, one little secret that may enable you to accomplish the feat. If you hold your free hand as far back as possible when pushing the object forward your centre of gravity will be positioned further back and you will find it easier to regain an upright position without falling flat on your face.

50. Show a Leg

Stand against a wall with your foot touching the skirting board and your left shoulder and head touching the wall. Now try to raise your right leg. As soon as you try to do so you will fall away from the wall. This is due to the fact that what you are really doing is changing your centre of gravity.

Try to lift that leg

Now try it on your friends. Bet them that they cannot lift their leg without coming away from the wall. It is a bet that you will win every time.

51. Touch Your Toes

Here is another example of how changing the centre of gravity can make an apparently simple task absolutely impossible.

Stand with your back touching a wall and your heels touching the skirting board. Now try to bend over and touch your toes without moving your feet away from the wall. You will fall over unless you know the secret.

The wall prevents you from bending forward

If you bend forward, as most people do, to touch your toes, you will fall forward, for you have altered your centre of gravity. Normally, when people bend down to touch their toes they counteract the change in balance by moving the tops of their legs backwards, but in this experiment the wall prevents you from doing this. You can, however, touch your toes if you bend sideways—always assuming of course that you are sufficiently fit to be able to touch your toes in the first place.

The secret is to bend to the side

52. Foot Stand

Stand against a wall with one foot touching the wall. Now try to place your feet together. You will find that it just cannot be done. Once again you have changed the position of your centre of gravity to produce an amazing result.

53. Balancing Bird

This will take a little time to make properly but it will amaze your neighbours when they see it perched on a tree in your garden.

First make a bird as follows. Make a hole in each end of an egg. Blow through one of the holes and the contents will splurge out on to a strategically-placed saucer. Use the contents for cooking.

Into one end of the shell stick a few feathers. On the other end glue a round ball made of dampened bread or light modelling clay. Glue a paper beak and eyes on to the head so you have a lifelike bird. Glue two matchsticks underneath the egg to look like legs.

You now need a length of stiff wire. The exact length will have to be established by trial and error for the weight

An unusual ornament for your garden

of your model bird will determine how much wire you will need. Bend one end of the wire at right angles to the rest and use a piece of sticky tape to attach it to the underside of your egg-bird.

Bend the bottom end of the wire at right angles and push it into a large blob of plasticine. To make the plasticine weight look more natural, glue the two halves of a walnut shell around it.

Stand your egg-bird on a branch in your garden and it will balance there, thanks to the plasticine weight, no matter what the weather and much to everyone's amazement.

54. Make a Stethoscope

Have you ever listened to your own heartbeat? You can if you make this simple stethoscope. All you need is a funnel, or the bowl of a pipe, and a metre or less of rubber tubing.

Fix one end of the tubing over the neck of the funnel. Place the wide end of the funnel over your heart and the far end of the tubing to your ear.

Listen to your heartbeats

The noise of your heartbeats enters the funnel and the tube carries the sound waves directly to your ear so you can hear your heartbeat quite clearly. If you have a watch handy you can count how many times your heart beats in a minute.

Try putting the funnel over things around the house; the radio, a watch, or an insect, and see how loud they sound through your stethoscope.

55. Shell Sounds

No doubt you have held a shell to your ear to hear the sea, but have you ever wondered what causes the noise that you hear? It is not, of course, the sea, but all manner of slight sounds that are going on around you that you cannot normally hear. All the minute sounds which would normally be dissipated in the air cause the shell to vibrate slightly. The small vibrations produced in the shell cause the air inside it to vibrate, creating the sound that you hear.

Listening to the 'sea'

56. Singing Glass

Take an ordinary wine glass and hold it by the base. Now wet the forefinger of your other hand and run it smoothly around the rim of the glass. With a bit of practice you will be able to produce a musical note. If you do not get it right the first time keep on practising, continually wetting your finger, and eventually you will get the glass to sing.

A smooth movement causes the glass to sing

The reason it does this is that the regular movement of your finger sets the glass vibrating and thus sound is produced. The purpose of the water is to enable a smooth and constant movement of your finger around the rim of the glass.

57. Whispering Glass

In the previous experiment you have demonstrated how a sound can be produced by running a wet finger around the rim of a glass. Can you now make a note come from a glass without touching it?

It sounds impossible, doesn't it? It is, in fact, quite easy. All you need is a little scientific know-how.

In addition to the glass you will also need an ordinary fork. A fork with long prongs is best. Place the glass on a table and hold the fork just above the table top. Click the prongs of the fork with your fingers or run a coin across the prongs. Because this action sets the prongs vibrating, a musical note will be produced, although it will not be very loud.

Now say that you are going to cause the note to travel from the fork to the glass. Click the prongs again and immediately touch the table top with the handle of the fork. The sound, louder this time, will appear to be coming from the glass.

What happens is that the vibrations from the fork cause the table to vibrate. This sets off even more vibrations in the air around the table, thus making the note sound even clearer. The glass? Well, to be honest, that does not have to be there at all. Because the sound is coming from all over the table it is difficult for the human ear to pinpoint its exact location. The glass gives the audience something on which to concentrate and the power of suggestion leads people to believe that because you said the sound would come from the glass that is, in fact, where it is coming from.

58. Wire Jumper

For this trick you will need two identical wine glasses, a thin piece of wire, and some water.

Pour water into the glasses until they are both about a quarter full. Rub one glass with a wet finger to produce a bell-like sound, as in the previous experiment. Do the same with the other glass. The note produced by each glass should be exactly the same for the experiment to work. If they are not, adjust the water levels until both notes are identical.

Now bend the ends of the piece of wire and rest it across the top of one glass. Rub the other glass to produce a sound and the wire on the first glass will start to dance up and down—even though you are nowhere near it!

This happens because the two glasses are in tune and when one vibrates it causes the other to vibrate in exactly the same way. It is these vibrations that cause the wire to jump up and down.

An example of the effect known as 'resonance'

59. Musical Spoon

As we have already discovered, the sounds we hear are, in reality, vibrations caused in the air around us. But, although we rely upon it to hear things, air is not a particularly good conductor of sound. Even a humble piece of string is a better conductor of sound—as you can prove with this experiment.

Tie a spoon to the centre of a piece of string about a metre in length. Hold the string at its ends and swing the spoon to hit a table. You will, of course, hear the sound produced.

Do the same again but this time hold the ends of the

String is a better sound conductor than air

string to your ears. Again you will hear the sound, but greatly magnified, for the strings are carrying the noise directly to your ear, whereas, normally, much of the sound is dissipated in the surrounding air.

60. Noisy String

Take a piece of paper (parchment paper is best if you can get some) and make a small hole in its centre. Push a piece of string through the hole and tie knots in one end of the string to prevent it from slipping out. Now place the paper over the end of a tin can from which the top has been removed completely. Use another piece of string or an elastic band to keep the paper in position.

Put a little bit of resin on your fingers, draw them along the string, and you will produce an amazingly loud noise. What happens is that your resined fingers, pulled along the taut string, cause the paper to vibrate and produce a sound. The tin can acts as a resonator and causes the noise to sound rather like a motor car hooter.

It sounds like a motor hooter

You can do this experiment without the resin, but the results may not be so good as your fingers will slide too easily over the string and will not produce sufficient vibration.

61. Bull-roarer

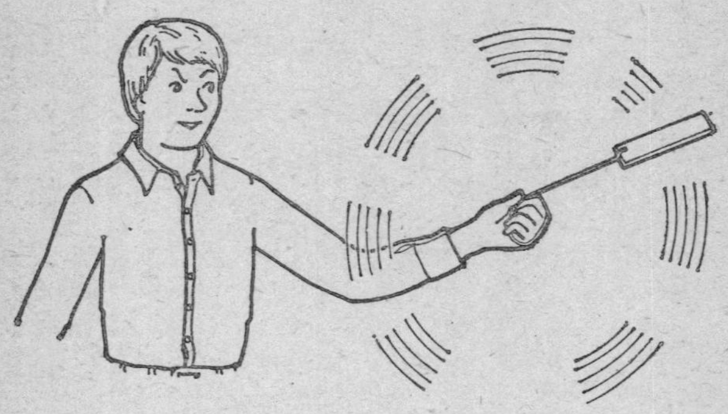

How aborigines frightened their families

This is a device that was once used by Australian aborigines to frighten their wives and children.

Take a piece of wood about two and a half centimetres wide and about eight or ten centimetres long, and bore a hole in one end of it. Tie a piece of string about a metre in length through the hole.

Hold the string in one hand and wrap part of it around a finger for safety. Now whirl the piece of wood around in the air, as fast as you can, and the bull-roarer will produce a loud groaning noise.

As you are whirling the string the wood rotates quite rapidly, twisting the string until it can twist no more. The string then untwists, causing the wood to rotate in the opposite direction. As it spins, the wood sets up vibrations in the air, which are the cause of the noise that you hear.

62. Keep It Turning

Here is another experiment accomplished by vibration. You will need a stick on which have been cut several notches. These notches should be equally spaced along the length of the stick.

You will also need a small propeller cut from paper, and a drawing pin. Push the pin through the propeller and into one end of the stick so it looks like the illustration.

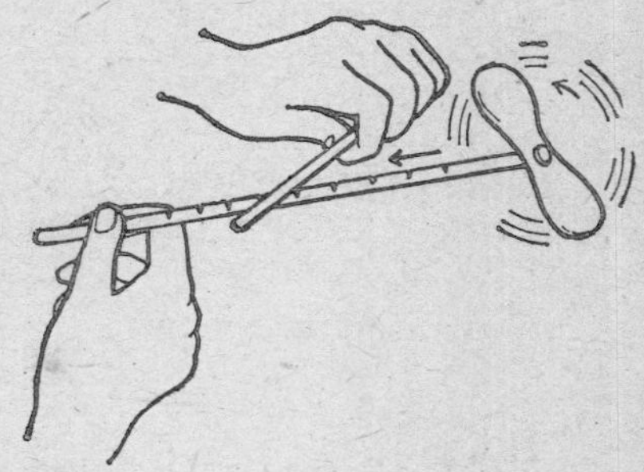

Scrape and the propeller turns

Run another piece of wood along the notches. Do this repeatedly and the propeller will begin to turn. This is due to the vibrations caused by the rubbing action being transmitted along the stick to the propeller. If you rub the notches in the opposite direction the propeller will spin the other way.

63. Direction Finder

Hang a horseshoe magnet from a piece of string and give the string a twist. The magnet will start to revolve but will eventually come to rest. When it does so, make a note of the direction in which it is facing and mark one of the poles of the magnet, so that you can tell one from the other.

Now twist the string again and watch as the magnet comes to rest. It will stop in exactly the same position as it did previously and the marked pole will also be in the same place.

In fact, one of the poles is pointing to the south and the other is pointing to the north. This is because the earth is itself a magnet and the poles of the hanging magnet are attracted to the same poles of the earth's magnetic field. Thus the north-seeking pole of the hanging magnet points to the north and the south-seeking pole points to the south.

64. Another Direction Finder

Take a large needle and stroke it several times in the same direction with one pole of a magnet. If you now place the needle on a small piece of card and float this in a bowl of water, the needle will turn the card until it is pointing in the same north-south direction indicated by the horseshoe magnet in the previous experiment.

The reason for this is that the continual stroking of the needle by the magnet has turned the needle itself into a magnet and this will seek out north and south in exactly the same way as any other magnet.

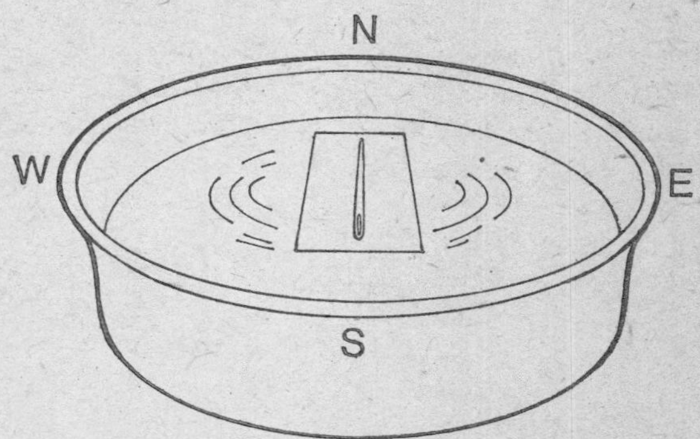

The needle will point to North

65. The Dancing Dogs

A little toy that was very popular some years ago, but which is not seen so often these days, consisted of two little dogs that danced. You could make the same toy yourself, for the thing that made them dance was magnetism.

Buy two small, flat magnets from your local hardware store and glue to the top of each one a cardboard cut-out of a dog. If you bring the dogs together on a smooth table-top they will sometimes rush towards one another, but at other times they will swing away as if they are dancing.

The explanation is quite simple. The north pole of a magnet will push away from the north pole of another magnet but if placed near the south pole of another magnet it will be attracted to it. In other words: like poles repel one another but unlike poles attract each other.

Once you know how your dogs are going to react when placed near to each other, you can get them moving about as if they were really dancing. You will need to have fast reactions though, for they will spin around and stick to one another if you are not quick enough.

66. Keeping Their Distance

For this experiment you will need a number of small corks, the same number of needles, a bowl of water, and a magnet.

Stroke each needle with the magnet so that they are themselves formed into magnets. Do this with the same end of the magnet in each case and stroke each needle in the same direction. Push one needle through each cork and float the corks in a bowl of water.

Hold all the corks together then let go—and they will begin to float apart. This is because the like poles are near one another and, as we have already seen in the previous experiment, like poles repel. But because there are several needles in the bowl they cannot be repelled too far before they come into contact with one of the others. In a few seconds they will sort themselves out and float at an equal distance from one another. Place another cork with a

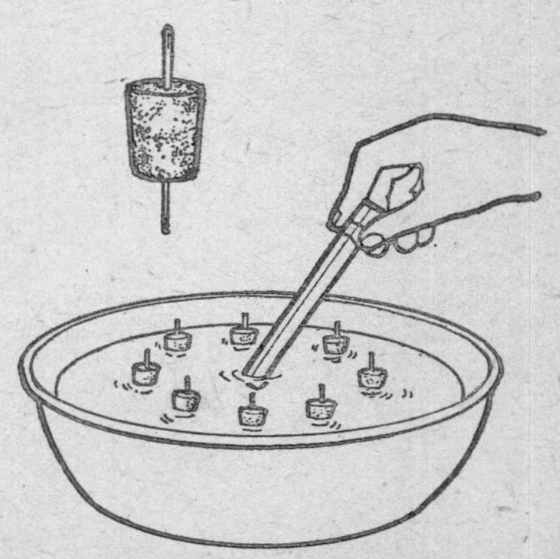

Use a weak magnet for this experiment

magnetised needle into a bowl and they will all rearrange themselves once again. Each time you add one, the pattern formed will change.

Now try holding a proper magnet near one of the floating needles and see what happens. With one end of the magnet the corks will all stay away at the same distance. Use the other pole of the magnet and one cork will be attracted to it but all the others will stay, forming a circle around the odd one.

67. Static Separation

Mix together some salt and some pepper. Can you now remove all the pepper so that only salt remains on the table?

One way you can accomplish this task would be to remove the pepper grain by grain. The only problem with this solution is that it is rather time-consuming and requires infinite patience. It is much easier to use science.

All you have to do is remove a plastic comb from your pocket and run it through your hair several times, or rub it briskly against your coat sleeve. This imbues the comb with a charge of static electricity.

Hold the comb above the salt and pepper mixture. Because the pepper is much lighter than the salt it will be attracted to the comb, like iron filings to a magnet, but the heavier salt will remain on the table.

It is possible that some of the grains of salt will also be attracted to the comb but these will not matter.

68. Bright Spark

Place a sheet of brown wrapping paper on a table. Now rub the paper with a stiff brush or soft woollen cloth. This rubbing creates a charge of electricity within the paper—and you can prove it in a most remarkable way:

When you have finished rubbing the paper, put a small bunch of keys in the centre of it and lift the paper by two diagonally opposite corners.

Ask someone to place his finger near the keys. When he does so he will be quite amazed, for a spark will flash from the keys to his fingertip.

A spark jumps from your fingertip

This experiment works best in dry weather and it is also important that the materials you use should be perfectly dry.

69. Unfriendly Balloons

Inflate two balloons and tie a piece of string to the neck of each balloon. Rub both the balloons with some cloth, or fur, as in the previous experiment.

Hold the end of each string and allow the balloons to hang down. From the results of the last experiment you might imagine that the static electricity would cause the balloons to stick together.

In fact, the opposite happens. Instead of attracting one another, the balloons spring apart in a most unfriendly manner. This happens because both balloons bear a similar charge.

When two similar charges are placed close together they push one another apart. This is what happens with the two balloons.

If you now place your hand between the two balloons it acts like a negative charge and the balloons are attracted to it. As soon as you remove your hand, the balloons spring apart once more.

A similar experiment can be conducted with two long strips of newspaper. Hold the two strips against a wall and rub them briskly, using repeated downward strokes, with the side of a pencil or a block of wood.

When the papers are held together at one end, the two lower ends will spring apart. As when using balloons, the papers will move inwards if you place your hand between them.

70. Bending Water

Have you ever noticed your hair crackling when you comb it? This is caused by static electricity and it can be used to perform some interesting effects. For example, did you know that you can bend water by electricity? This is how you do it:

First, turn on a tap, so that it produces a slow and thin, but steady, stream of water. Now comb your hair vigorously to produce a charge of static electricity. Bring the comb near to the stream of water and the water will start to bend towards the comb, attracted by the electricity.

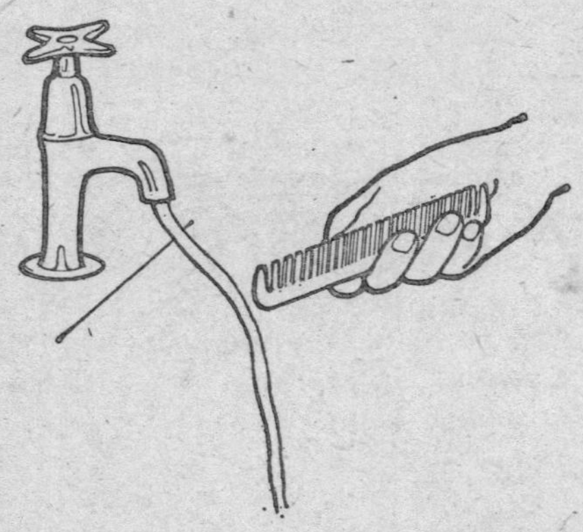

Static electricity bends the water

You can do the same thing with a balloon that has been rubbed with wool or with many other things made of plastic. Be careful that you do not actually touch either the water or the tap or the experiment will not work.

71. Butterfly Dance

Here is another simple experiment that proves that electricity can be generated by friction.

From a sheet of tissue paper cut out three or four butterfly shapes. Tie a thin thread to each butterfly and use a piece of sticky tape, or a blob of plasticine, to fix the other ends of the threads to a piece of cardboard.

Now get a sheet of brown paper and rub it briskly with a clothes brush or a cloth. Hold the paper above the butterflies and they will jump into the air, attracted by the static charge you have produced, and dance at the end of their threads.

The butterflies are attracted to the paper

As with all experiments using static electricity, the items used must be perfectly dry. They usually work best on a dry day. You can get even better results if you warm the brown paper a little before carrying out the experiment.

72. Hot and Cold

If you tell your friends that something can be both hot and cold at the same time they will not believe you. But you can prove it with this experiment.

All you need are three bowls of water. The first bowl contains hot water, the second luke-warm water, and the third icy cold water. Get a volunteer to put one hand in the cold water and the other hand in the hot water. Do not have the water *too* hot, for this is a scientific experiment, not a torture.

Tell him to keep his hands in the water for about five minutes, during which time, as he cannot run away without taking his hands out of the water, you can show him one or more of the other experiments in this book. At the end of five minutes he is to put both his hands in the luke-warm water and he will feel it both hot and cold at the same time. To the hand that was in the hot water, the luke-warm water will seem cold, and to the other hand it will seem hot because each hand had become accustomed to the previous temperature.

73. The Vanishing Elephant

The famous magician, Harry Houdini, often used to wave his magic wand and make an elephant disappear. He used a real elephant, but you can do the same trick with the elephant drawn on this page.

Close your left eye and hold this book about fifty centimetres from your face. Look at the picture and you will be able to see both the elephant and the magic wand. Concentrate your gaze on the magic wand and move the book slowly towards your face. All of a sudden the elephant will disappear. Keep moving the picture near your face and eventually the elephant will appear once more.

The explanation of this mystery is that there is a blind spot in the human eye. It is situated at the point where the optic nerve from the brain enters the back of the eyeball. When the light rays from an object fall upon this spot, no message is sent to the brain. Normally this does not cause us any bother because the other eye, seeing the same thing from a different angle, makes up for this temporary loss of vision. When one eye is closed, as in the above experiment, the thing at which we are looking can seem to disappear.

74. Rabbit in the Hat

A favourite trick of magicians is to pull a rabbit out of a hat that has been proved to be empty. Here is an optical illusion that will enable you to do something similar.

On a disc of card draw a top hat. On the other side of the card, but upside down, draw a half a rabbit. You will have to experiment to get the exact positioning for this rabbit. Make two holes in each side of the disc and thread some string through the holes as shown in the illustration.

Hold one string in each hand and twirl the disc round and round so that the strings twist. Pull your hands apart slightly and the strings will untwist rapidly, causing the disc to spin around. As this happens, people watching will see the rabbit *in* the hat, for the disc is spinning so fast that the eye cannot react quickly enough to its movement. In effect,

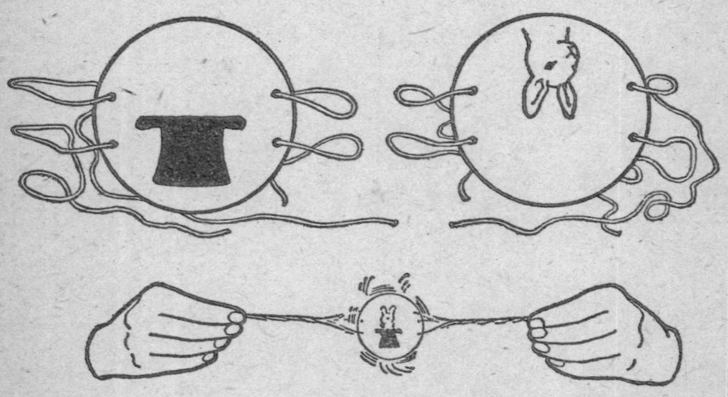

Spin the disc and the rabbit is in the top hat

everyone sees both sides of the disc at the same time, so the rabbit appears to be in the hat. When the disc stops spinning, you can show the picture of the top hat and state that the rabbit has vanished, but do not, of course, show the other side unless your fingers are concealing the half rabbit.

75. Jumping Finger

Close one eye and then hold one forefinger, or a pencil, up at arm's length. Look at the finger and open the closed eye as you close the other eye. The finger will appear to jump from one side to the other.

If you continue to open and close each eye alternately as fast as you can, the finger appears to be imbued with a life of its own for it is now leaping rapidly from side to side.

76. Pin Point

With a pin, make a small hole in a sheet of paper or card.

Now close one eye and look at the head of the pin holding it about ten centimetres away from your face. You will find the pin extremely difficult to see—especially if you focus your view beyond the pin.

But when you place the card between your eye and the pin you will be able to see the pin clearly. This is because the small hole acts as a lens.

77. Re-light

Light a candle and allow it to burn for a few minutes. Now blow out the flame and hold a lighted match a short distance above the wick. The candle will immediately re-light!

The reason for this is that the hot vapour given off by the candle comes into contact with the flame of the match. The flame travels along this vapour to the wick and re-lights the candle. If you allow the liquid wax around the base of the wick to go cold it is impossible to light the candle in this way.

The flame travels down the fumes to the wick

78. Weight Lifter

Thread a metre of strong string through the hole in the centre of an old cotton reel. Tie one end of the string to a small weight and the other end of the string to another weight, up to ten times as heavy as the first. If you cannot find suitable weights almost anything will do, provided they are not too large—a couple of potatoes or stones, for example. If you use objects that do not have a ring or a hole through which you can tie the string, make sure that you tie them on securely, or the smaller one might fly off when you try the following experiment.

We are going to make the small weight lift the heavier weight. That may sound impossible but all you have to do is hold the cotton reel in your hand with the small weight hanging over the top. Now shake your hand and start the small weight spinning round and round in the air. As you spin it faster and faster, you will see the small weight pull the larger weight up towards the cotton reel.

This happens as a result of the centrifugal force being exerted by the small weight. This force occurs because all

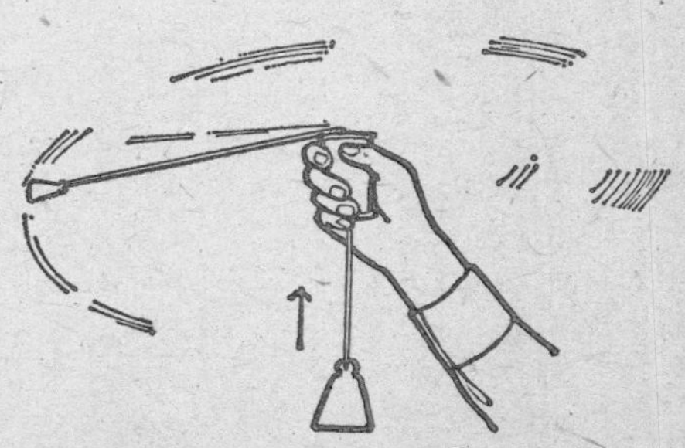

The faster you spin, the higher the weight will go

objects, once set in motion, tend to continue in a straight line. In this instance, the small weight tries to keep going straight but the string prevents it, and, as a result, the small weight tries to move away from the centre and pulls the larger weight with it.

79. Tears for Two

Take a sheet of paper measuring about ten centimetres by about 25 centimetres and make two tears in it, one from either side, to divide the paper into thirds. Stop tearing when you are about three centimetres from the opposite edge. When you have done this the piece of paper should look like the one shown in the illustration.

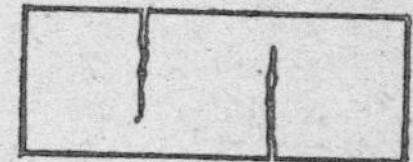

Hand the sheet to a friend and ask him to hold it with one end in each hand. Ask him now to pull his hands apart and try to tear the paper into three pieces. As you have already done most of the work for him he will think that you are quite mad for requesting such a simple task—

It will not tear into three pieces!

until he tries to do it. No matter how carefully he pulls his hands apart, he will always end up with two pieces of paper, never three.

This is due to the fact that no matter how carefully you do the original tearing (in fact your friend could do it for himself if he thinks you are cheating), the tears will never be exactly the same length and there will be minute differences in the way that the tears are formed. Also, there are irregularities in most paper that make it thicker in some places than others, and this means that the amount of pull required to complete the tears you have already made will differ according to the varying strengths in the paper. So, although it looks like a simple task, the odds are stacked up against your friend achieving it.

80. Winter Warmth

All you need for this experiment are two pieces of cloth, one of which is a light colour, preferably white, and the other dark, preferably black. Oh, and you also need a garden full of snow—which rather restricts the number of chances that you will have to try the experiment.

Early in the morning, place the two pieces of cloth on the surface of the snow a short distance apart. Leave them there for the rest of the day. If you think that they might blow away, place some small weights on the corners, but try to make the weights identical for each piece of cloth or they may affect the result of the experiment.

When you look at the pieces of cloth in the late afternoon you should notice a remarkable thing—the light coloured cloth is still on the surface of the snow, assuming of course that the weather has not changed drastically and all the snow has melted, but the black cloth will have caused the snow beneath it to melt.

This experiment was first tried by the eighteenth century American scientist Benjamin Franklin, and the strange result is achieved because light materials reflect the sun's heat whereas dark substances absorb it. Thus the dark cloth is warmer and so it melts the snow underneath. It is for this same reason that people who live in hot countries wear white robes, to reflect the sun's heat and keep them cool, and why you should wear dark clothing during the winter to keep you warm.

81. Going Through

If you take a cube of ice from the refrigerator and squeeze it, the cube will begin to melt. It is the pressure exerted by your hand, as well as the heat from it, that causes this to happen.

Make a large block of ice by freezing some water in a long container. You could, for example, use the normal ice-making tray from the refrigerator with the divisions removed. When the ice block is formed, rest it across two bricks. Loop a length of wire over the block and tie the ends to a heavy weight, such as another brick.

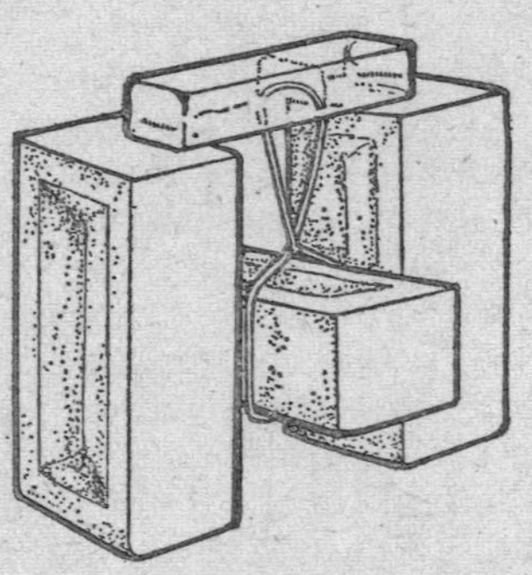

An example of 'regelation'

After a short while you will notice that the pressure of the wire is melting the ice where it is in contact with the wire. Slowly, the wire will cut its way right through the block of ice. But the block will not be cut in two, for as the wire melts the ice and moves down through it, the water runs around the wire to refreeze above it and so the block stays in one piece. This effect is known to scientists as *regelation.*

When doing this experiment it is a good idea to place a cloth or a tray on the floor to catch the drips of water—and the brick when the wire has gone right the way through the ice.

82. Scientific Separation

Mix some salt and pepper together and then challenge your friends to separate one from the other.

One method of accomplishing this, using static electricity will be found on page 95. But here is another way that is just as effective but which is accomplished by utilising a completely different scientific principle.

The principle we are going to use is that of relative density. This is the density of a substance compared to the density of water. If the relative density is greater than that of water the substance will sink, if it is less great the substance will float. The relative density of salt is higher than that of pepper, so all you have to do is tip the mixture into a glass of water. The salt sinks to the bottom and the pepper floats on the surface, so the two are separated, as required.

83. Egg in Suspension

You probably know that it is easier to float in the sea than it is in a swimming pool. This is because the sea is denser than fresh water, due to the salt contained in it. Perhaps you have even seen pictures of people floating in the Dead Sea which contains so much salt that it is almost impossible to sink.

Here is an experiment you can try, to prove that salt water will support a floating body much more readily than fresh water.

To perform this experiment you will need an egg, a glass jar, some water, and plenty of salt.

Fill the jar with water and place the egg into it. The egg will sink to the bottom of the jar. Do the same thing again, but this time first dissolve as much salt as you can in the water. To get the maximum amount of salt into the water, it is a good idea to heat the water, as the salt will then dissolve in it more readily. When the water is cooled, put it back into the jar, and drop the egg in again. This time, because the density of the water is greater than previously, the egg will float.

A rather amusing variation of this experiment can be tried using both salt and fresh water. Half fill the jar with salt water. Now very carefully pour in some fresh water. Put the egg into the water and it will neither sink nor float, but will remain suspended at the mid-point, supported by the salt water which no-one but you knows is there.

84. Crazy Chalk

If you dip a piece of chalk into acid the two will react together to produce bubbles of carbon dioxide. This you can demonstrate to your friends in a most fascinating way.

Pour some vinegar into a shallow non-metal tray and then place a piece of chalk rock in the vinegar. The acid in the vinegar reacts to the calcium carbonate in the chalk to produce bubbles of carbon dioxide. These are produced so rapidly, that the chalk will start moving crazily around the tray, propelled, although you friends will not know this, by the bubbles of gas being produced.

This experiment will not work with the sort of chalk used in schools.

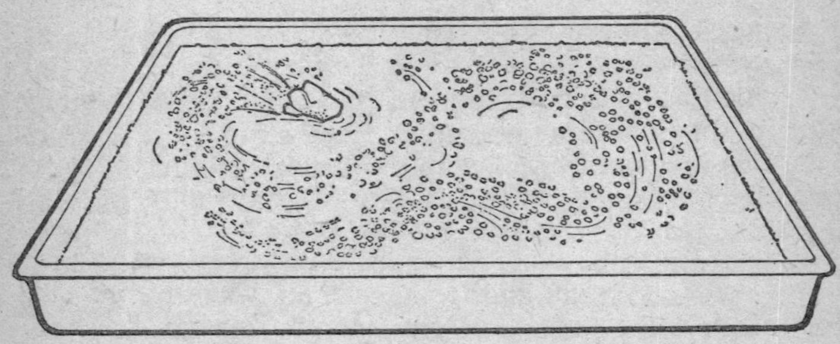

85. Mothball Magic

If you place a mothball in a jar of water it will sink to the bottom, but if you add a couple of special ingredients to the water you can make the mothballs float up and down in a most amazing way.

The special ingredients are baking soda and vinegar. Pour equal quantities of each, about two tablespoons should be about right, into the jar of water and give it a good stir until all the baking soda has completely dissolved. Now put in a few mothballs—and they will sink to the bottom. No, don't worry, the experiment has not failed. Leave it for an hour or so and see what happens.

The vinegar and the baking soda react together to produce carbon dioxide bubbles. These bubbles will cling to the mothballs and will make them rise to the surface. When they get there the carbon dioxide dissolves in the air, the mothball loses its support, and sinks to the bottom again. In due course it will collect some more carbon dioxide and rise to the surface to repeat the action. And, as all of the mothballs are doing this, and will continue doing it for some time, you will have quite an unusual toy to show your friends. The mothballs bounce up and down in the water as if they cannot make up their minds whether to stay at the bottom or on the surface of the water.

86. On the Wing

Have you ever wondered how an aeroplane, that is much heavier than air, can fly? As the aeroplane moves forward, air rushes under and over the wing. Due to the way that the wing is shaped, the air going over the top has further to travel than that going under the wing. Therefore the air on top of the wing is travelling faster than the air below and this results in a partial vacuum that lowers the air pressure above the wing. Because of this the wing is forced upwards.

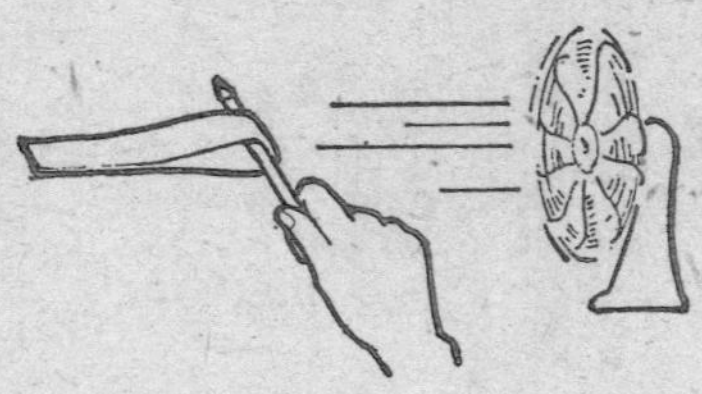

Now let us see if we can prove it. First you must make a wing. To do this, bend a sheet of thin card into the wing shape shown in the illustration, and glue the ends together. Push a pencil through the wing and hold it in front of a fan and you will see the wing move upwards into a horizontal position.

87. Acrobatic Coin

Place a small coin such as a halfpence on the table, a short distance away from a saucer. You will have to try this out in private first, to establish the correct distance between the coin and the saucer. Now challenge someone to blow the coin into the saucer. Yes, that's right, *blow* the coin into the saucer.

It sounds impossible, but you, being a scientist, will be able to do it by reducing the air pressure above the coin. As we have seen, a reduction in air pressure pulls things up, and this is what will happen to the coin. All you have to do is to blow sharply and directly on top of the coin. You will need some practice to get this right every time but you must remember to blow directly on top of the coin. If you blow over or under the coin it will not work. The onrush of air lowers the air pressure above the coin and it will flip into the saucer of its own accord.

88. Underwater Volcano

Fill a small ink bottle with cooking oil to which a small quantity of vegetable colouring has been added. Fit a cork, with a small hole bored through it, into the neck of the bottle. Place the full bottle in the bottom of an old bowl and then use plaster of Paris, clay, or plasticine to construct a miniature mountain around the bottle. Make a crater in

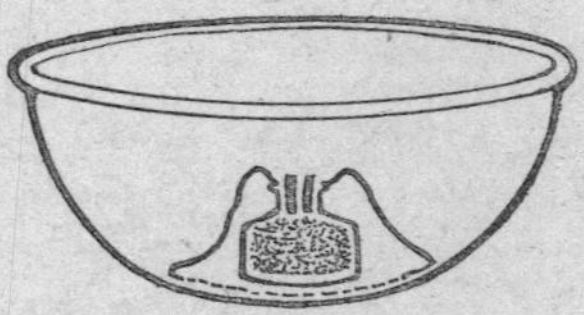

Build a plasticine volcano around the bottle

the top of the mountain just like that of a volcano so that the hole in the cork is exposed.

Watch the volcano 'erupt'

To make the volcano erupt, all you have to do is pour water into the bowl until it covers the crater. Give the bowl a little nudge and red oil will begin to rise from the crater, just like fire from a volcano. It looks very impressive, especially to those who do not realise that this is simply a demonstration of the different densities of oil and water. The oil, being lighter, rises to the surface.

89. Taking the Temperature

For this experiment you will need a bottle with a cork, a drinking straw (transparent if possible), and some plasticine.

First make a hole in the cork and push the straw into it. Fill the bottle with water. It is a good idea to add some colouring to the water. You can do this with poster paint, vegetable colouring, or ink.

Put the cork and straw into the bottle and then use the plasticine to seal around the neck of the bottle and around the hole in the cork.

You will find that if you now place the bottle in a warm place the level of the coloured water in the straw will rise.

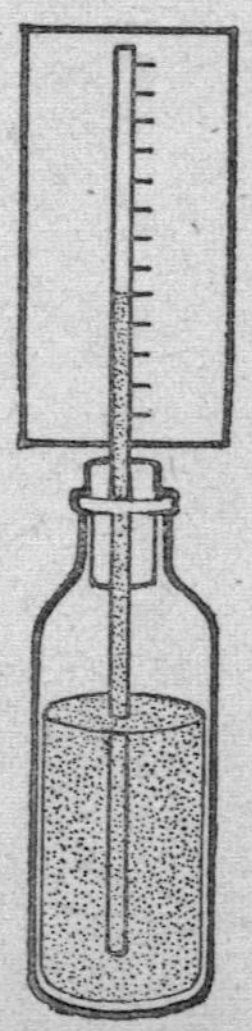

If you place it in a cold place the water level will go down. This is because when water is warmed it expands, and when it is cooled it contracts.

What you have made in fact is a simple thermometer. If you mark the straw with lines you will be able to compare the temperature changes from day to day or in different rooms of your house.

To make your thermometer even more sophisticated, glue a piece of card to the straw. Borrow a real thermometer and expose it, and your home-made thermometer, to different temperatures. By consulting the real thermometer you can find out the actual temperature. Write that temperature on the card alongside the water level in the straw. Do this with several different temperatures and you will build up a scale on the card. You can now use your thermometer to find the warmest and coldest places in your house. Or you could record the temperature each day and see how it varies with the weather.

90. Colour Change

Pour some water into a glass and then add just enough ink to turn the water blue. Into another glass put a few drops of household bleach (bleach is poisonous, so be careful) and you are ready to show an amazing trick.

Show the blue liquid to your friends and say that you are going to use your magic powers to turn the blue ink into water. Pour the blue liquid into the second glass and the water will turn clear, just like ordinary water.

There is, of course, no real magic in this trick for it is simply brought about by the chemical reaction of the chlorine in the bleach with the blue water which is poured on to it. But if your friends do not know this then it looks like real magic.

One word of warning: Do not drink either of the liquids and make sure that you wash the glasses out *thoroughly* after demonstrating the experiment.

91. Create some Crystals

Buy a packet of epsom salts from your local chemist or supermarket and dissolve as much as you can in a jug of hot water. There should be about two glassfuls of water in the jug. When you have dissolved all you possibly can, pour the solution into two tumblers, and stand them side by side. Now place a length of cotton across the tumblers so that each end is hanging well down inside each tumbler as shown in the illustration. Place a saucer under the thread between the tumblers. Leave this set-up somewhere safe for about a day while you try some of the other experiments in this book.

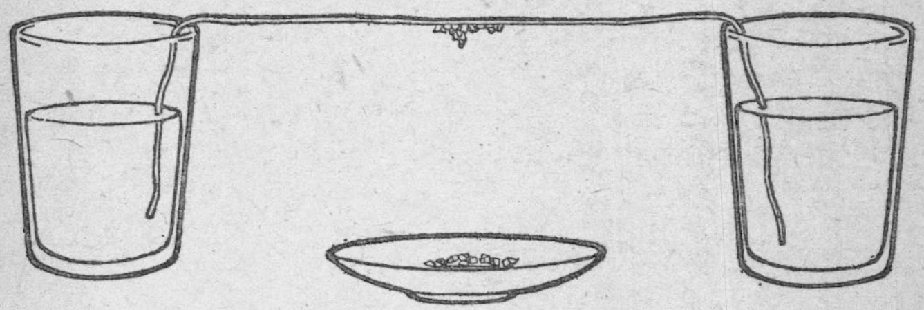

As the solution drips from the thread, crystals are formed

Next time you look at the thread you will find that a number of fascinating crystals are hanging from it. You will also find some crystals in the saucer underneath the thread. The crystals were formed in much the same way as stalactites and stalagmites are formed—by the drips coming from the thread. (Of course, you do not have to be told that the solution moved up the thread by capillary action, so it will not be mentioned.)

Each time you try this experiment, the form that the

crystals take will be different. You could also try the same experiment using a solution of ordinary salt or sugar and see how the crystals vary.

92. Shadow Ghost

To do this experiment you must first cut out the shape of eyes, nose, and mouth from a sheet of card. You also need a strong light source—a table lamp with the shade removed should prove sufficient.

Ask someone to stand in front of the light so their shadow is thrown on to the wall. Place the cardboard on a mirror and then hold it behind the lamp. You may have to manipulate the mirror slightly but after a bit of practice you will find you can direct the light quite accurately. When you do this you will find the light reflected from the

cut-outs on the cardboard is superimposed on your friend's shadow so it looks as if he has glowing eyes, nose, and teeth.

This experiment can be really quite spooky but you can add to the effect with the help of another friend.

In this case you will need two mirrors and two cut-outs. From one piece of card just cut out the eyes and the nose. From the other sheet of card you cut out the mouth. You place your card on a mirror and your friend does the same with the other. You both stand behind the lamp as before. Once again someone is asked to stand in front of the lamp to cast a shadow. Your friend and yourself position your cards so the cut-out portions are reflected on to your victim's shadow as before. If one of the cards is now moved you can achieve quite a ghostly effect.

For best results this experiment should be done using dark-coloured cardboard and a clear bulb. The results are not nearly so effective if you use light-coloured card and a pearl, or frosted bulb.